Koala!

Fun Facts about the World's Cuddliest Marsupial

An info-picturebook for kids

Susan Mason

Table of Contents

Koala 1

Marsupials 3

Name 6

Habitat 8

Appearance..10

Koala Menu.......................................13

Koala Night Life...............................16

Life Cycle 18

Koala Cooling System.....................22

Koala Noses 24

Communication 25

Fingerprints 27

Koala Care..28

Glossary 33

From the Author 34

Other Funny Fauna 35

Koala

Many people think that the koala is one of the cutest animals in the world. Koalas certainly look cuddly.

Koalas are very cute

Well-known for their large round head, large furry ears and big black nose, they are often called koala bears. You might even have a stuffed animal koala "teddy bear" on your bed!

Although people may refer to koalas as "koala bears" due to their similar appearance, they aren't actually bears at all.

Koala "teddy bear"

They do in fact belong to a group of animals called marsupials that includes kangaroos, possums and bandicoots.

Marsupials

Marsupials are the group of mammals that often have a pouch, like wallabies and kangaroos.

Koalas have a pouch, like kangaroos

The pouch is very important for marsupial babies (known as "joeys"), as they are born when they are at an early stage of development and need to stay in a safe place to continue to grow.

Joeys are blind, blond, hairless and have only slightly formed limbs when they are born. Cleverly, they find their way into their mother's pouch without seeing! They have to rely on all their other senses. Once they have arrived in the pouch, they can develop further in safety.

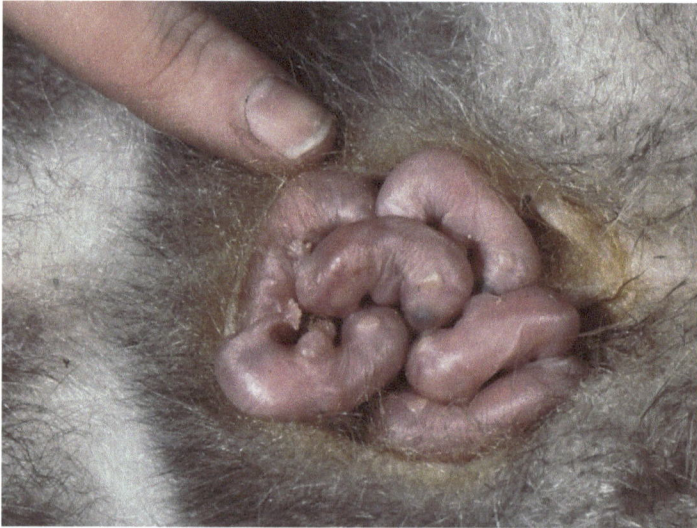

Baby possums in their mother's pouch

About two-thirds of marsupials live in Australia and its neighboring islands, such as New Guinea. Where else do marsupials live? We can find them in North, South and Central America. So amazingly, koalas are related to many other animals.

Examples of other marsupials include possums, bandicoots, quolls, wombats, tree kangaroos, antechinus, dunnarts, bettongs, quokkas, sugar gliders, Tasmanian devils and Virginia opossums.

Koalas are related to bandicoots

Name

Koala, in the Aboriginal language, means "no water." The Aboriginal people so-named these animals because they never seemed to drink. But how is this animal able to survive without water?

If you have a pet cat or dog, you will notice how they drink water from their water bowl. This is very different from how koalas generally absorb fluids.

Many animals, like cats, lap water

Firstly, as they move around very little and sleep for such long hours, koalas don't really need all that much water. But secondly, they receive most of their hydration through eating the leaves of plants that are already water-rich.

Koalas receive water through eating plants

Sometimes, however, you might see koalas climbing down from trees to drink from a waterhole to get any extra water they need, especially in very hot summers.

Habitat

What's tall, green, and a prime spot to find a koala enjoying his lunch? It's a eucalyptus tree. Eucalypts are iconic Australian trees, sometimes called gum trees.

These cute, furry koalas are only native to Australia, which makes them quite rare. Some mature eucalyptus trees where koalas can live look very mighty and tall indeed.

Eucalyptus trees

Eucalyptus plants come in all sorts of shapes and sizes. In fact, there are over 700 species of eucalyptus. Most eucalyptus plants are trees, but some are shorter shrubs.

Koala clinging to a tree

The reason you will see koalas in these trees is because they are tree-dwelling animals. Similar to the way birds are at home in trees, that is the way you could say koalas live in trees.

In fact, our little furry friends hug the trees so tightly, that it is practically impossible to pull them off!

Appearance

Now, let's move on to what exactly koalas look like. Featuring fluffy ears, round heads, and spoon-shaped noses, koalas are famous for their adorable faces.

Koalas are famous for their facial features

Koalas have long, sharp, specialized claws ideally suited for climbing trees, with two "thumbs" placed opposite the three "fingers" of the same paw.

Koalas have two thumbs and three fingers!

Their back paws have four digits and a large clawless toe for balance. Koalas also have rough pads for additional grip during climbing. That's probably why you won't see koalas falling out of trees!

With stout bodies and short tails, koalas can grow to between two and three feet high (60-90cm), which is as tall as a small child. Southern koalas are typically larger than northern koalas. Northern koalas weigh 9-20 pounds (4-9kg), while southern koalas weigh 15-29 pounds (7-13kg).

Koalas actually come in a variety of fur colours too, including grey-brown, silver-grey, golden and even chocolate-brown. These colours can provide koalas with camouflage protection, like a chameleon, against tree bark.

A chameleon uses camouflage to avoid being seen

Koalas in Queensland (on the hotter, north-east coast) are lighter in colour and have less fur than those further south. This probably helps to keep them cool.

Koala Menu

Koalas are unique animals that can survive on a diet of eucalyptus leaves, sometimes called gum leaves, which are tough, fibrous, and low in nutrition. They've got some cool physiology to help them, like a long caecum, which branches off from their large intestine.

Eating eucalyptus leaves

The caecum is packed with millions of bacteria that help break down eucalyptus leaves, letting koalas absorb nutrition from them. As you can imagine, koalas take their sweet time digesting food, to get the most out of it. Their slow metabolism helps them do this.

Eucalyptus leaves

Koalas are pretty choosy when it comes to food, sticking to just a handful of eucalyptus species. Not any old gumtree will do for them!

Eucalyptus leaves contain toxins that are harmful to most animals but interestingly, koalas can detoxify these chemicals. Trees growing on less fertile soils tend to have higher toxin levels, so koalas avoid them.

Using their sharp front teeth to cut their food and special molars to grind it effectively, adult koalas munch on around half a pound to a pound (225-450g) of leaves each day,

Koala Nights

Koalas are nocturnal animals, which means they are most active during the night. But even at night they will take short naps! As eucalyptus leaves take a lot of energy to digest, koalas need more sleep than most other animals. All in all, koalas can sleep up to a whopping 20 hours each day!

Koalas need lots of sleep

They only get moving when they really need to, nestling themselves into the fork of a tree the rest of the time. So, while koalas might occasionally move around during the day if disturbed or when needing to find a new tree, their primary activities are reserved for the night-time, when they will feed, move around and interact socially.

Life Cycle

Koalas generally reproduce once a year. The new-born joey weighs less than a twenty-fifth of an ounce (1g) and looks something like a pink jellybean. It is blond, blind and hairless, and looks very different from the cute, fluffy, little bundle that it will become later.

Young koala

Once inside the safety of its mother's pouch, it takes several months for the joey to grow and develop, drinking its mother's milk, until it finally shows its little face to the world.

As soon as it begins its diet of gum leaves, the young koala grows at a much faster rate. At first, the young koala cuddles into its mother's belly for warmth and shelter. It also rides on its mother's back.

A joey on its mother's back

Soon, the young koala will begin to make short trips away from its mother, becoming more adventurous as it grows bigger and stronger.

Baby koalas learn to climb trees as part of their development. Initially, they cling to their mother's back or belly, observing and copying her movements. As they grow, they start practising on their own.

Joeys learn from their mothers

From 12 months onwards, slowly but surely, koala joeys leave their mothers to find their own home ranges. That's when life gets harder for young koalas because they have to find their own territory near other koalas — somewhere with the right tree species of yummy gum leaves to eat.

Grown-up koalas find their own territory

Koalas typically live up to 15 years in the wild and a bit longer in captivity. However, their age can de-pend on factors like habitat quality, diet and threats from predators or human activities.

Koala Cooling System

Seeing a koala hugging trees is just not an adorable sight. Hugging trees actually has an amazing practical purpose! It's no secret that the weather gets very hot in Australia.

Australian summers can be very hot

A summer temperature of around 100 degrees Fahrenheit (37 Celsius) is common in many regions, which is very hot indeed!

So how do koalas stay cool? Well, they mainly keep cool by hugging trees. In the leafy shade, hugging trees helps regulate their body temperature, as the bark of the trees is much cooler.

Hugging trees keeps koalas cool

Koala Noses

Koalas also have an incredible sense of smell which they rely on heavily when choosing the best eucalyptus. They can tell the difference between different types of eucalyptus trees and even identify the freshest and most nutritious leaves to eat.

Koalas can smell out the best eucalyptus leaves

Communication

Koalas are quite vocal and make different sounds to communicate. Male koalas produce deep, loud bellows, especially during the mating season.

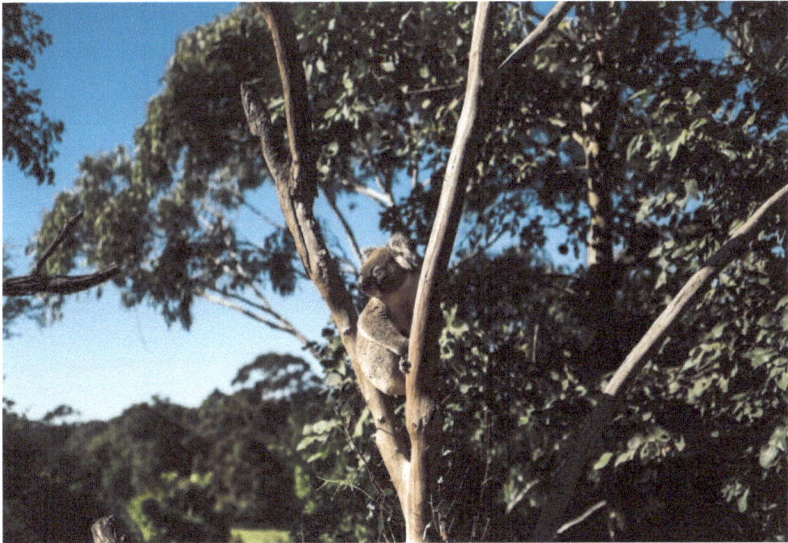

Male koalas call for a mate

These bellows can be heard from quite a distance and are used to attract females and intimidate other males. Joeys often make high-pitched squeaks, especially when they are calling for their mothers. Koalas can also produce a high-pitched scream when they are in distress or feel threatened.

Fingerprints

And yes, it is true that koalas have fingerprints! In fact, their fingerprints are remarkably similar to human fingerprints. This similarity is so striking that even under a microscope, it can be challenging to see the difference between the two. For koalas, having fingerprints helps them grasp and manipulate eucalyptus leaves.

Koalas have fingerprints!

Koala Care

Did you know that koalas are "shrinking"? They aren't a big as they used to be, due to some of the challenges they face from natural dangers and human activities, and they are also decreasing in numbers as well.

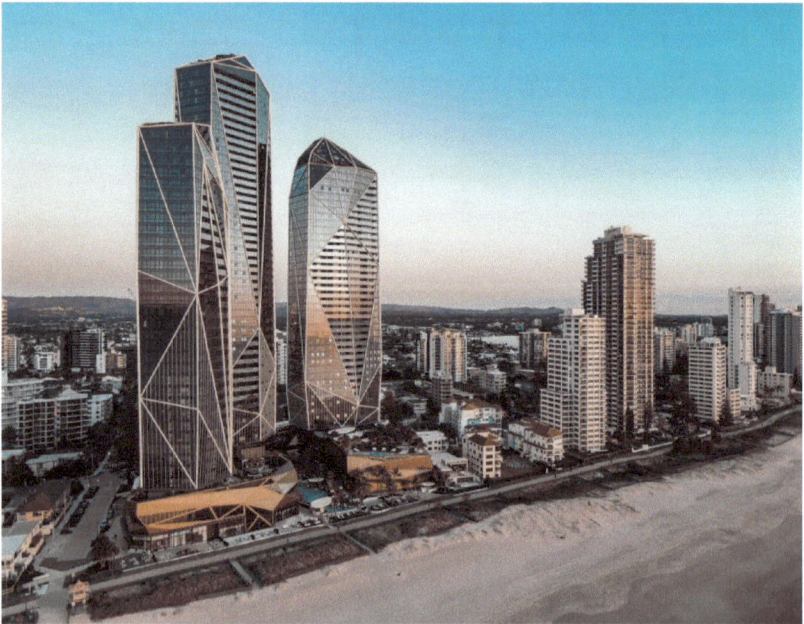
Development can destroy koala habitat

From habitat loss to bushfires, koalas are threatened in many ways. These circumstances prevent koalas from growing to their maximum size, so they are smaller than they used to be.

The biggest threat to koalas is habitat loss. Much of the koala's habitat in Queensland overlaps with areas where significant clearing has occurred, so building can take place.

Eucalyptus sapling

One way to help with this problem is to plant native trees. This restores koala habitats, which is very important as koalas rely on eucalyptus trees for food and shelter.

The second biggest reason why koalas are fewer in number is that cars can hit them when they are on the road.

Sadly, in South East Queensland, many koalas are killed each year by motor vehicles. So, motorists need to drive carefully, especially at night when koalas are moving around. Koalas need to cross roads too!

Koala alert road sign in Australia

Dog attacks are another major threat to koalas. Responsible pet owners can help by keeping their dogs indoors, or tying them up, at night.

Koalas also have natural predators, like snakes, dingoes and foxes. Birds like wedge-tailed eagles and powerful owls tend to prey on the younger koalas.

The powerful owl preys on koalas

However, with the many actions being taken to protect koalas from natural and man-made dangers, like habitat conservation, driver and pet-owner awareness, we can be confident our koala friends will not only survive, but thrive into the future.

With protection, koalas can have a bright future

Glossary

Aboriginal – the original people to inhabit an area

Fibrous - having fibre

Hydration – process of absorbing water

Iconic - viewed as a representative symbol

Intestine – long, tube-shaped organ in the abdomen that completes the process of digestion

Metabolism – processes that turn food into energy so the body can operate

Microscope - instrument used for viewing very small objects

Nutrition – consuming food

Population - all those living in a particular place

Predator - an animal that hunts others

Species - a kind or sort

Territory - an area of land, sea or space belonging to a country, person or animal

Free Offer

If you would like a free Koala Fun Worksheet, just go to the link below:

https://bubblepublishing.com/free-koala-fun-worksheet/

From the Author

If you have enjoyed this book, it would be great if you could leave a review on Amazon, letting me know what you think.

Just go to the *Koala!* purchase page on the Amazon website, and add your review at the bottom of the page.

I would love to hear from you!

Susan Mason

Other Funny Fauna

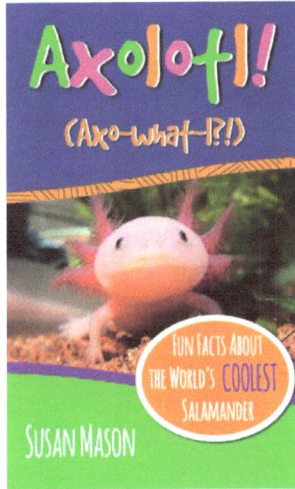

In this salamander book you will discover:

- The axolotl's special healing ability
- It's ancient link with mythology
- How the axolotl reproduces two ways
- Its camouflage ability
- And much more!

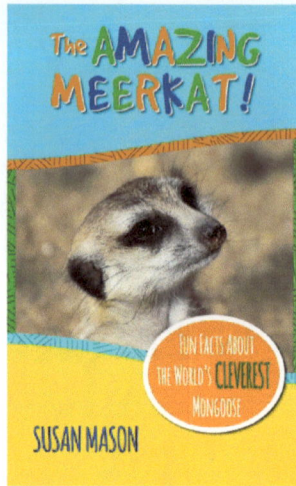

In this mongoose book you will discover:

- How meerkats deal with poisonous prey
- The meerkat's amazing tunnelling ability
- Meerkat babysitters
- And much more!

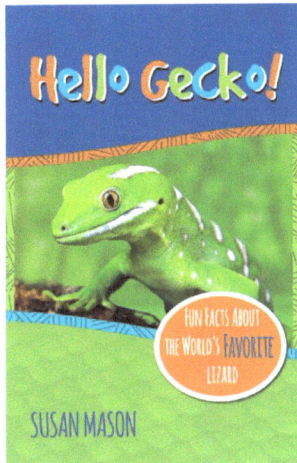

In this lizard book you will discover:

- The gecko's special "stickability"
- The unique way these lizards communicate
- How geckos have four ways to reproduce
- And much more!

Available on Amazon.